Sam

by Alan Levine
illustrated by Phyllis Pollema-Cahill

Scott Foresman
is an imprint of

Glenview, Illinois • Boston, Massachusetts • Chandler, Arizona
Upper Saddle River, New Jersey

Every effort has been made to secure permission and provide appropriate credit for photographic material. The publisher deeply regrets any omission and pledges to correct errors called to its attention in subsequent editions.

Unless otherwise acknowledged, all photographs are the property of Pearson.

Photo locations denoted as follows: Top (T), Center (C), Bottom (B), Left (L), Right (R), Background (Bkgd)

Illustrations by Phyllis Pollema-Cahill

Photograph 8 ©Dorling Kindersley

ISBN 13: 978-0-328-50696-5
ISBN 10:   0-328-50696-6

3 4 5 6 7 8 9 10 V0N4 13 12 11 10

Sam can quack.

Sam can come to Jack.

Sam can go that way
on the rug.

Sam can swim in my tub.

Sam can have a snack.

Ducks are living things. They need food and water to live. There are many different kinds of ducks. Ducks live all over the world.

8